MORE POWER TO YOU!

21 Workable Tips That Will Make You More POWERFUL!

Herbert G. Hicks, BCE, MBA, PhD
Chairman and CEO
Entech Systems Corporation

MORE POWER TO YOU!

By

Herbert G. Hicks, BCE, MBA, PhD

To Jane, Caren, Carl, Cole,
Grant, Jordan, Justin and Jana

CONTENTS

A PERSONAL NOTE TO MY READERS...

So far, in my career spanning more than 40 years, I have been an engineer in technical businesses, taught management in universities, worked as a management consultant, served as an Air Force officer, and practiced as a manager and executive in several businesses and other organizations.

The common denominator--the energy--in all these activities was power. In every case power was exercised over me, and I exercised power over others.

Like the subject of sex for the Victorians in the late 19th and early 20th centuries, power somehow seems to have gained a bad reputation. Better not to talk about it; it's not a proper subject for nice folks, the attitude sometimes seems to be. No doubt, dictators and despots often have abused their power, causing us sometimes to think that power is bad.

But power clearly is necessary to do *anything*. Every bad thing is done with power; that's true. Yet every good thing also requires power to be accomplished. I think the more we know about power, the better and more ethically we will use it. So let's have a go at it.

MORE POWER TO YOU!

Herb Hicks

P. S. I haven't provided "answers" for the questions at the end of each "tip." The questions are meant merely to help you think about and reach your own answers about your issues related to each "tip."

Power Tip #1

POWER IS THE GAME OF LIFE

Do you want more power? Of course, you do! You, I, and every one else want more power. That's right, POWER! We all have some power, and EVERYBODY WANTS MORE POWER!

Power isn't optional. We don't just want it. Power is absolutely required for *everything everybody* does. Taking a breath, pushing a stalled car, making money, sitting by a rushing mountain stream, going to heaven, feeding starving children, saving the world from sin, conquering another nation, and doing *anything* else in life *all* require power. The idea that some people want power, and others do not is false. Everyone wants power, just for different, individual reasons.

Perhaps the idea that everyone wants power seems obvious. It *is* obvious once you have thought about it. But it was not obvious to me before I started writing this book. Is it obvious to you?

I want power to write a successful book (about

POWER!). I also want power to eat, power to see a good movie, and power for limitless other things. There might even be a part of me that wants to be "Emperor of the Universe," to have all power, to be God.

What are some of the things for which you want more power? Many things, no doubt. You might want more money. You might want a promotion. You might want to empower the homeless.

We've wanted power all our lives. We'll always want more power. That's just being human. Neither you, I, nor anyone else can do anything without power.

Kurt wants to bathe, dress, and go to a movie.

Nto wants to be protected from crime.

Cole wants to be president of his class.

Jane wants to paint a beautiful flower and be invited to join the Artists' Guild.

Grant wants to study turtles and other critters.

Elaine wants to be elected to the County Commission.

Jumba wants to double his sales.

Chen wants to have heart surgery.

Maria wants to go to heaven when she dies.

Klonsky wants relief from his terrible kidney-stone pain.

You want to be successful and make a lot of money.

You want to marry the person of your dreams.

You want to have three children.

You want to go to Switzerland.

You want good health.

You want to be attractive to others.

You want to be respected in your community.

And on, and on, and on, every need or want requiring power to satisfy.

Power is a common denominator of life. We must have power to live and to attempt to get all the things we want. I want more power. You want more power.

Understanding your power and how it works will make you even more powerful. That is, you can use your power to get additional power. That's what this book is about-- more power for you!

POINTS TO PONDER

1. List ten things you want that require you to have more power to get them. How, if at all, can you get the power necessary to have each thing you want?

2. How much power would it take to satisfy you completely? How does your desire for more power compare to the desires for power of other people you know?

THE BOTTOM LINE, TIP #1:

The entire "game of life" is played with power.

Power Tip #2:

POWER IS THE UNIVERSAL CONSTANT

When you are thinking about...	You might not always realize it, but you are thinking about the POWER of...
God	God
Enlightenment	Enlightenment
The Sun	The Sun
War	War
Peace	Peace
Splitting the Atom	Splitting the Atom
The Pacific Ocean	The Pacific Ocean
The USA	The USA
The Diamond Cartel	The Diamond Cartel
Middle East Oil	Middle East Oil
American Industry	American Industry
The State of California	The State of California
Ohio State University	Ohio State University

African-Americans	African-Americans
The Rocky Mountains	The Rocky Mountains
The City of Seattle	The City of Seattle
The Chicago Bulls	The Chicago Bulls
Silicon Valley	Silicon Valley
Ford Motor Company	Ford Motor Company
Federal Reserve Bank	Federal Reserve Bank
New York, NY	New York, NY
Mathematics	Mathematics
Acme TV Repair	Acme TV Repair
House Flies	House Flies
The VP of Marketing	The VP of Marketing
Sunnydale High School	Sunnydale High School
A Chevy Corvette	A Chevy Corvette
Your Family	Your Family
Your Work Place	Your Work Place
Your Friends	Your Friends
Your Job	Your Job
You	You
Your Clothes	Your Clothes
Your Knowledge	Your Knowledge
$100	$100

If you can name it, you can talk about the power of it. Power is everywhere and in everything. Power is inherent in all of creation. Power is the universal constant.

POINTS TO PONDER

1. Have you ever been told (either verbally or nonverbally) that having lots of power is bad? If so, who told you this? Where do you think they were "coming from"?

2. It you became more powerful does that mean that someone else became less powerful? Why?

3. Are you somewhat uncomfortable with the idea that everything contains power? Why?

4. Is there a fixed amount of physical power in the universe? Is there a fixed amount of social or organizational power in the universe? Why?

THE BOTTOM LINE, TIP #2:

Everything you can think of involves power.

Power Tip #3:

THE UNIVERSE IS POWER

Everything that happens in the Universe is an expression of and exercise of power. Nothing happens without power. Power is the energy that makes the Universe, your company, other organizations, you, me, and everyone else "go." Power is universal.

Perhaps the ultimate expression of power is the creation and operation of the Universe. (That is, unless there are, have been, or will be additional Universes about which we do not know.)

The Earth--our island home in space--is one of about a dozen planets revolving around the Sun, which appears to be a typical Star in our Galaxy, the Milky Way.

There are estimated billions of stars in the average Galaxy. Then there are estimated billions of Galaxies. So the estimated total number of Stars (the Sun is one) is billions in each Galaxy *times* billions of Galaxies--more than 1,000,000,000,000,000,000--a truly mind-blowing number. Surely, the Universe is an expression of indescribable power.

Your power is small compared to the total power of creation. However, chances are you have a lot of power, perhaps much more than you realize. You might never have recognized or appreciated all of your power. Probably, you have much more power than you use.

Power created the Earth. Power created you and me. Power makes the Earth revolve around the Sun. Power created the Sun--that enormous "hydrogen bomb" in our sky--which is the source of almost all power on Earth.

You and I have power. We were created by power. *Everything* we think or do requires power. We'd be dead without it!

Power is energy! Life is energy! Life is power!

POINTS TO PONDER

1. Have you ever thought that everything that happens in the Universe requires power? What does this thought mean to you? Do you feel powerless compared to the awesome power of the Universe? How do you think others feel about this?

2. Do you and others seek more power to gain more personal control of the awesome, sometimes frightening events of life?

3. Whose power would you most like to have: The Pope, The President of the United States, or Bill Gates (the wealthiest person in the world)? Why?

4. Who has the most power over you. Are you comfortable with that relationship? What changes would you like to make?

5. Try to think of three things you recently did that did not require power. Can't do it, can you?

THE BOTTOM LINE, TIP #3:

Power is everywhere and in everything.

Power Tip #4:

POWER IS ABILITY

If I have the ability to influence your thoughts, feelings, or behavior, then I have power over you.

If I have the ability to get you to call this customer, but not that one, I have power over you.

If I have the ability to promote, demote, hire, fire, or raise your pay, I have power over you.

If I have the ability to detain--even for a moment--you, I have power over you.

If I have the ability to give you pleasure by playing golf with you, I have power over you.

You also have power in many areas, perhaps different from mine.

You have power over your infant daughter. (Of course, she also has power over you, if she can make you get up and give her a bottle in the middle of the night!)

You have power to live in the desert, if you wish.

You have power to give or to withhold your affection.

You have power to decide the company for which you will work.

You have power to decide whether or not you will continue reading this book.

You have power to decide to take or not a course on taxation.

You have power to give a raise to an employee.

Power sometimes is unfair, exploitive, unreasonable, and "not nice." So, we often use terms such as "influence," "pull," "authority," "juice," and so forth, perhaps trying to make power seem less "dirty" or less "offensive."

Such "sanitizing" terms, we might think, disguise, "soft-pedal," or hide power, perhaps making power seem less "bad." Certainly, power often is used to do bad things. But, remember we must use power to do every good thing, too.

Power is simply the ability to do something. Whether that something is good or bad involves authority issues-- morals, opinions, values, ethics, laws, and so forth--our next topic.

POINTS TO PONDER

1. Do you think that power itself or having power is evil?

2. How much power do you have? Is it enough? Why? How much power would you like to have?

3. Is there a part of you that wants to be King or Queen of the Universe? Would it take that much power to satisfy you? Would you truly be happy then? (I'm sorry to report that a study showed that lottery winners are not happier!)

4. What are three ways you are not effectively using your power? What can you do about them?

THE BOTTOM LINE TIP#4:

Power is the ability to do something, anything, everything!

Power Tip #5:

AUTHORITY IS RIGHT

Power is the ability to do something; authority is the right to do that thing. Power is the bullet that comes out of the barrel of a gun. Authority says whether or not the shot is justified.

One can have power to do something. However, whether one has the right to do that thing is another matter. One might or might not have the authority to do it. Authority is the moral, ethical, legal right to do something.

Authority is legitimate power. Laws, regulations, company policies, customs, values, ethics, morals, and habits are some of the ways individuals and organizations define authority.

Just because a person, a company, or a nation has the power (ability) to do something doesn't mean they have the authority (right) to do it. Likewise, a person or an organization might have the authority (right) to do something, but lack the power (ability) to do it.

Dealing with this tension between power and authority

greatly occupies the minds, souls, and bodies of everyone throughout their lives.

You must decide whether you have the authority (right) to discipline your child. You might have the power (giving him a severe beating, for example) to do it, but lack the authority (a severe beating might be illegal) to do it that way.

Think of atomic energy, a vast source of physical power. Atomic energy inherently is neither good nor bad. Yet the uses of atomic energy--in bombs, for example--can be good or bad, depending upon who is making the value judgment.

The same is true of economic and all other kinds of power. They are not inherently bad, but their use can be bad (lack authority).

Your supervisor might have the power (take it out of the petty cash account) to give you a raise, but lack the authority (that's not a proper use of petty cash) to do it that way.

Citizens must decide how much authority to give their governments. Religions create authority by defining sins, values, and morals. A baseball league publishes the rules (permitted and not-permitted behaviors) of the game. Your company says you cannot sexually harass your workers.

The concept of "authority" is what makes us "civilized." Know, respect, and use it wisely!

POINTS TO PONDER

1. Think of an example in your life when you had more power than authority. When you had more authority than power. How did you feel (frustrated, confused, bitter, angry, excited, pleased, etc.) about these imbalances of your power and authority? What did you do?

2. To what extent is your nation redefining its authority systems? That is, how are its values, morals, ethics, and laws being changed? Will this process ever he completed? Why?

3. Does your work organization clearly define you authority and power? How and how not?

4. Which comes first: power or authority? Why? What gives someone the right to say what is right? What would organizations look like with power but no authority?

5. What is the authority (value, ethic, moral, law, etc.) that you most want to change? Why?

<u>THE BOTTOM LINE, TIP #5:</u>

Authority is the right to do something.

Power Tip #6:

ACCOUNTABILITY IS STEWARDSHIP

When you exercise power you are the steward, substitute for, or surrogate of the person or organization that gave (delegated) power to you. You act as a delegate for or in the place of the person, God, "system," organization, or manager that gave you power and authority.

The person or organization that delegated to you expects you to report on your stewardship or use of that power and authority. When you received delegated power and authority you explicitly or implicitly agreed to account for how well or poorly you used them.

What did you do with this power? Should you be given more power? Should some of your power be taken away from you? Accounting to the source of your power lets that source evaluate you to answer such questions.

Generally, accounting to a "higher" source is not fun. There is a part of each of us that does not want to account-- to have to report on how well we "performed."

Perhaps there is a part of each of us that wants to be God. Maybe we sometimes go a step farther and think that we ARE God. Some psychologists and some religions say we do this. "God doesn't have to account; if I were God I wouldn't have to account." So my thinking might go. Yet the truth is neither you nor I is God. Too bad, isn't it?

Members must account to "higher" (in the organization's structure or "chain of command") members of the organization for the organization to he successful. Members account as to their stewardship of powers that have been delegated to them.

An organization without accountability works poorly, if at all. Such an "organization" is not freedom. It is anarchy. It is chaos. *Every* nation, company, other organization, and person grants power or freedom *within limits*. You must account for your use of that limited power. And if you exceeded the limited power granted to you, you also must account for your use of that "extra" power.

Some people describe themselves as anarchists. They think we do not need government, so they think they should not have to account to any government because its existence is illegitimate in the first place. But no such idealistic system exists; it never will.

Each of us would like to be totally free to do our own thing. But the essence of civilization is effective accounting to the organization at every level. So-called "flexible" organizations still have structures and limits that will be relied upon when being "flexible" works poorly, or not at all. Everyone in a successful organization must account for the power given to him or her.

POINTS TO PONDER

1. Do you find it difficult to account for your use of powers that have been given to you? Think of several instances where you have had such difficulties. Think of several instances when accounting has been easy for you.

2. Is it easier for you to account to higher authorities or for you to require those to whom you have given power to account to you? If there's a difference, why?

3. What areas of government, religion, and business require too much accounting?" Which too little? Can rigid systems for accounting give a sense of security to some people? Explain.

THE BOTTOM LINE, TIP #6:

Be ready to account for the power delegated to you.

Power Tip #7:

RESPONSIBILITY IS DUTY

Do you do your duty? Do the members of your organization who are accountable to you do their duties? Are you and they responsible?

Doing your duty means doing what you, your God, and others with authority expect you to do.

Persons are responsible when they recognize and accept their duties, when they have the necessary power, and when they pursue their duties to completion. Responsibility is an inner, felt, and accepted obligation to account to the authority that delegated power and authority to you. Responsibility simply is doing your duty.

Whether a person is responsible depends upon an internal willingness to "do the right thing." Of course, that person must have been delegated appropriate power and authority.

In many respects you cannot make another person responsible. Being responsible or not is an expression of one's personality, which is largely fixed for most adults, who rarely will make significant personality changes.

You can delegate power and authority to someone, and you can require that person to account to you. If the person does not account satisfactorily or at all you can take corrective actions. For examples, you can counsel, admonish, reprimand, or discharge the irresponsible person.

Many people do not act responsibly. There are times when all of us fail to be responsible; we just don't want the burdens of being responsible.

Much has been made in America about a supposed decline in "family values." That's a way of saying that some persons think others are not doing their duty, failing to be responsible. (Of course, it is much, much easier to talk about others' irresponsibility than to face up to one's own irresponsibility, isn't it!)

Consider a parent who refuses to take care of a young child. Is the parent failing to do his or her duty? Many people would say, "yes." Is this a breakdown of responsibility? Again, many would agree.

Responsibility is essential in organizations ranging from families, to small businesses, to schools, to religions, to massive companies, and to governments.

POINTS TO PONDER

1. When was the last time you behaved irresponsibly? When did someone last behave irresponsibly toward you?

2. How can you be more responsible? How can you help others to be more responsible? Is it easier for you to see and criticize another for being irresponsible than it is for you to see and criticize your own irresponsibility? Why?

3. What are the relationships among values, customs, duties, laws, and responsibilities? Who determines all these things? Which of these need to be changed? Why?

THE BOTTOM LINE, TIP #7:

Be responsible; be the example. Others might follow you.

Power Tip #8:

POWER, AUTHORITY, ACCOUNTABILITY, AND RESPONSIBILITY WORK TOGETHER

Every successful human organization must have a workable mix and balance of power, authority, accountability, and responsibility.

First, the organization has enough power (resources) to do the things it exists to do. Power has many forms: physical, social, political, religious, economic, and so forth.

Second, the organization has authority. That is, its power is legitimate and it is used legitimately. Environments affirm and support what they see as desirable organizations and activities. Likewise, environments discourage or punish organizations whose activities are seen as undesirable.

Third, the organization has accountability. It reports as to its stewardship of the assets (power) provided to it by its environment and by "higher" authority.

Fourth, the organization has responsibility. It uses as power (resources) in ways approved by its members and by its environment. A responsible organization has a "conscience." It builds up its environment. When it does, the environment will "bless" it, and support its activities.

Successful organizations have good balances of power, authority, accountability, and responsibility. All four work together.

Because an organization's resources and its environments change, the organization must dynamically adapt to these changes. If it fails to do so, it will die. Few buggy whip manufacturers still exist. Also, you won't find any makers of steam-driven automobiles. They had their niche in now out-of-date markets--their time "in the sun." But the needs and wants of their environments changed. Every organization must change to be renewed, or it will die.

POINTS TO PONDER

1. Consider an organization of which you are a member. Does it maintain dynamic, successful balances of power, authority, accountability, and responsibility?

Which of these four factors is weakest? Which is strongest?

2. Identify three organizations whose environments "punished" them. Then identify three whose environments supported them.

3. Think of a short-lived and a long-lived organization. Does managing power, authority, accountability, and responsibility differ in these two organizations? If so, how?

4. Is your work organization risking its life by poorly managing power, authority, accountability, or responsibility? If so, how?

5. How would you advise your boss to improve your organization's managing of power, authority, accountability, and responsibility? What can you do by yourself?

THE BOTTOM LINE, TIP #8

Managing dynamic, productive balances of power, authority, accountability, and responsibility gives successful organizations.

Power Tip #9:

DELEGATING POWER CREATES LARGE, COMPLEX ORGANIZATIONS

Suppose you work in a large organization. Most of your power was delegated to or given to you "from above." Your manager passed power down to you. Similarly, her power largely had been passed down to her from her manager. That is the classic process of delegation of power.

Through delegation, power is given to you--created for you--from your manager, who got power from her manager, who got power from his manager, and so on. When the delegation process works effectively, everyone in this "chain" has the power required to do her or his job.

When your manager delegates power to you does she have less power than before? No, she simply tells you to use some of her power. You do your job, using the power she delegated to you. As her delegate, you act in her place. She can reclaim the power if she wishes.

Power delegation produces the hierarchy or structure of

an organization. In an ideal structure every person has the necessary power to do her task. Power, authority, accountability, and responsibility are perfectly known and balanced throughout a "perfect" organization.

Delegation does not always work perfectly, however. For example, when you make mistakes, your manager is accountable to her manager for your mistakes.

A perfect organization never existed. Even if it had, it would almost immediately become imperfect because the environment within which the organization "lived" is always changing.

Still, a hierarchy is essential; an organization won't work well without one. In fast-changing environments, successful organizations have flexible and nimble structures, able to adapt their hierarchies to rapid environmental changes, including their markets.

Successful organizations create power when their products (tangible and intangible) are more valuable than their costs. Then they make "profits," either financial or non-financial. That's why we have organizations; we hope they make profits.

POINTS TO PONDER

1. When is the last time someone delegated power to you? Who did it? Was that delegation a proper exercise of that person's power? Was is done clearly? Did you properly acknowledge your acceptance of that power? Was the delegation successful?

2. When is the last time you delegated power to someone? Who was it? Was that delegation a proper exercise of your power? Did you delegate clearly? Did that person properly acknowledge his or her acceptance of that power? Was the delegation successful?

3. Imagine a world without delegated power. How would it "look"? Would it work? Why or why not? Would you like to live in such a world? Why or why not?

THE BOTTOM LINE, TIP #9:

You and your organizations will become more powerful if you use your present power effectively.

Power Tip #10:

POWER ALWAYS FILLS A VACUUM

Sometimes random chaos exists; there is no effective organization. The costs of chaos are so high--due to uncertainties, conflicts, anxieties, random behavior, and other reasons--that there is enormous pressure "to organize," which requires the exercise of power. So when chaos exists, power comes in--sometimes "rushes in"-- to fill the vacuum, to overcome the chaos.

We cannot chose whether we will have a power system in an organization, only how and by whom the power will be exercised. And if you don't like an existing power system you might--as in a war--die trying to change it.

Much of your power is latent, or informal. Your latent power is the power you have that has not explicitly been delegated to you, but is implicit in you, your position, and the situation.

Your total power is like the electricity in your home.

The electricity you use is "active power." Usually, a lot more electricity is available. That unused power is "latent power." Often, you can greatly increase your active power by using more of your latent power. Almost everyone has a lot of latent power.

Suppose you see a drowning child while you are walking by a lake. You try to rescue the child, using your latent power. No one specifically delegated to you power to save this drowning child. If you try to do so, you use your latent power.

Powerful people skillfully and assertively use their latent power. They expect that their effective use of their latent power will be accepted, supported, and rewarded. Often it is.

On the other hand, you might be reluctant or afraid to use your latent power. Using latent power sometimes "back-fires."

You might be criticized or punished for using your latent power. "Pushy," "aggressive," "excessive," "improper," and "illegal" are some terms others might use to describe your use of your latent power.

If the results of using your latent power are seen as

good (according to the evaluator), then that use will be supported. Likewise, bad (according to the evaluator) results might be criticized, opposed, and penalized.

Your failure to use your latent power can be seen negatively. "No initiative," "fear of failure," "too set in her ways," are some terms that might be used by a person who thinks you have failed to use use your perceived (by them) latent power.

Successfully using (according to the evaluator) latent power gets positive reactions. "Takes initiative," "goes out of his way to be helpful," "always tries to give the customer more than he expects," might be positive reactions to your use of latent power.

POINTS TO PONDER

1. During a massive, extended electrical failure in New York City, traffic became almost hopelessly snarled. At one (perhaps many) intersection, a plain citizen stepped forth with his flashlight, and began directing traffic. Apparently, everybody willingly accepted his directions. How was this a use of his latent power? Did he fill a power

vacuum?   Why were people willing to follow his directions?   Did they see his exercise of power as an acceptable alternative to unacceptable chaos?   Would you have stepped forth and directed traffic like this man?   Why or why not?

2.   Have you ever exercised power by "filling a vacuum"?   Could this be a legitimate way for you to become more powerful?

3.   Caren, a ten-year old, and a number of adults were watching television in a ski lodge in Colorado.   In the middle of a program, Caren got up and changed the channel.   Soon, all the adults began to leave, without comment. How were Caren's actions examples of using her latent power?   Did she have the authority to change the channel? Did she have the power? What would you have done in this situation? Why?

4. Ajax Company is into "Total Quality Management (TQM)." One of the principles of TQM is to "give the customer more than she expects." How might following this principle be an example of using latent power? To what extent does your work (or other) organization encourage (or expect) you to take initiative--to use your latent power? How could you and your organization improve in this area?

THE BOTTOM LINE, TIP #10:

Become more powerful; fill a power vacuum!

Power Tip #11:

ORGANIZATIONS CREATE VALUE

Why do we have organizations? Because we expect them to make "profits." That is, we expect the value of their outputs to be greater than the cost or value of their inputs. Of course, the inputs and outputs usually have different dimensions. Money (a tangible thing) you pay for a security system gives you a feeling of safety (an intangible thing), for example.

Organizations are so important that we simply could not have modern life without them. High-tech life and organizations are inextricably interwoven. In fact, we usually think of modern life in terms of the organizations that provide it. Without complex organizations, we would quickly revert to primitive living. We would do without many comforts and benefits we automatically expect.

A successful organization generally creates net assets that are worth more than their production costs. Organizations typically do not merely rearrange or redistribute assets, although they also can do that.

You might say: "That's obvious; I already knew that." But are we usually really aware of the great extent our modern life depends on the productivity of our organizations? The fabric of modern life truly is woven with organizations. We are unwilling to do without the benefits that only organizations can give us.

Organizations also distribute or redistribute assets. Robin Hood, for example, took things from the rich, and he gave them to the poor. Much of politics, economics, ethics, morals, and religions are involved with "distribution" or "fairness" issues.

Sometimes some people "win" from an organization while others "lose" from the same organization. That is, an organization might provide net additional benefits to some participants at the same time it provides negative net benefits to other participants.

In a "perfect" organization all participants gain from their involvement in the organization. Yet, you might--as an individual--be a net "loser" in a particular organization that generally is seen by others us successful.

Can you seriously consider doing without organizations? I can't. We even need organizations to fight other organizations with which we do not agree!

POINTS TO PONDER

1. Think of an organization with which you have been involved that was successful for you. How did the organization produce "outputs" more valuable to you than your "inputs" to the organization? How did you measure the outputs of the organization to you and your inputs to it? Ask yourself the same questions about an organization that was unsuccessful for you.

2. Think of an organization that was successful to you, but was unsuccessful to another person. Also, think of an organization that was unsuccessful to you, but was successful to someone else. Are your and the other person's conflicting evaluations due to different values or opinions you and they hold? Why?

3. Think of an organization that is more interested in the "fair" redistribution of assets than it is in the production of additional assets. Is there a proper place for such an organization? Could the redistribution of assets itself create more net value? If so, how? If not, why?

THE BOTTOM LINE, TIP #11:

Successful organizations produce more than they cost.

Power Tip #12:

SYNERGY IS POWER

Here is the great secret of the enormous power of organizations: Organizations have a synergistic effect. Synergy often allows an organization to be profitable, financially or otherwise.

The fire in your fireplace does not burn with only two pieces of wood. Add a third piece, and the fire leaps! The result (fire) with three pieces of wood differs both quantitatively and qualitatively from the result (no fire) with two pieces. That's synergy.

The third piece, which is a 50% increase in the amount of wood, does not produce merely 50% more flame than the two original ones. Rather, the third piece is necessary, together with the original two pieces, to produce any flame. In this case, we must have "an organization" of three (or more) pieces of wood to get any flame. That's synergy.

Consider a cake. We can make a cake by combining flour, eggs, shortening, milk, flavorings, and maybe some other ingredients. The finished cake--if it's good--is worth much more than the sum of the value of all the ingredients. Even when we add the costs of the mixing bowl, cake pan, oven, and our labor, the cake might--again, if it's good--be worth more than all its costs, tangible and intangible.

If our cake is successful, we have made a profit. That is, the value of our finished goods (the cake) is more than our costs. Our "organization" of all the tangible and intangible things that went into making the cake made a profit.

An atomic bomb explodes if it has a "critical mass," enough explosive material within a certain limited space. It will not explode with less than a "critical mass." That's synergy.

Just as in these physical examples, synergy works in successful human organizations. We make a profit when we organize and combine our human and other resources so that the value of the products produced by the organization exceeds the costs.

Synergy causes successful human organizations to produce more or better things--tangible or intangible--than could be produced without synergy. Because of synergy, the benefits of a successful human organization are greater than the mere sum of its parts.

Like for an atomic bomb, organizations allow us to assemble synergistically human and other resources to get "critical masses." For example, in the Gulf of Mexico, oil is being produced from under water which is thousands of feet deep. This requires combining many millions of dollars worth of equipment and many specialized human skills.

Give me $1,000,000 and ten workers, and I certainly could not get the oil out of the earth from under that deep water. Give me $100,000,000 and 500 workers of my choice, and I might get the oil. Combined successfully synergistically, we might create a "critical mass" of technology and people to produce oil at a profit.

The organizational process of creating "profits" (where the things produced have more value than their cost) is the synergistic effect of organizations. Synergy might cause an input of 2 units of a resource (a form of power) + an input of 3 units of another resource (a second form of power) to produce a result (a third form of power) that typically does not equal five.

The output in this example might equal 5, a break-even result. Or the sum might be 4, a loss. Or it might be 6, a profit. Or the sum might be X, Y or Z. That is, the units of value created by the synergistic effect can be of different dimensions from the inputs.

Indeed, the outputs of most organizations usually are different kinds of things than were the inputs. This is a reason why it often is difficult to evaluate the effectiveness of individuals and organizations. Standards, tastes, and objectives differ among individuals, parts of organization, and the whole organization.

Synergy often allows us to break out of the limiting idea that 2 + 3 always equals 5!

POINTS TO PONDER

1. Do you understand the concept of synergy well enough to explain it to someone else? Why do we sometimes associate the terms "magic" and "secret" with synergy? Is there something here that appears to defy logic? If so, what?

2. Think of an example of positive synergy from your experience. Also think of an example of negative synergy from your experience. Should we always seek positive synergy? Why?

THE BOTTOM LINE, TIP #12:

Enlist synergy in your army of productivity!

Power Tip #13:

PHYSICAL STRENGTH IS POWER

The elemental, most basic form of power is physical strength.

Suppose I'm a five-year-old whose life is shattered by the arrival of a baby brother. I'll beat up on him. I might even want to kill him, and perhaps I would if I could. Short of murder, however, I'll kick him and hit him; I'll try to use all of my power to exterminate him, at least to get him out of my life.

Chances are my parents will use some form of physical power to try to keep me in line. They might hit me if I hit baby brother. At the least, they might pull me away from him. They might close me in my room as punishment. Or they might make me sit in the corner, and pull me back into it when I try to get out.

Adults fight, too, just like young children. Perhaps the main difference is that the weapons adults use are much more deadly.

Gangs use power. Mobs use power. Despots use power. Many bad things use physical power.

Yet many good things use physical power, too. Breaking in a door to rescue a child from a fire uses physical power. Pumping water to irrigate strawberries uses physical power. And when the Braves beat the Yankees, they did it partly with physical power.

Thinking about using, and actually using physical power is often ugly and destructive. Yet. the "good" use of physical power produces many of the things we value. When potentially destructive power is channeled to constructive use we can say that the power has been "sublimated." Better to lose a soccer game than a shoot-out with the rival "tribe," isn't it?

Today, America is the world's only physical superpower. That physical, military power is available to be used throughout the world. It affects the economic, political, religious, and social lives of billions of people. Truly, physical power always has been, is, and will be important in everyone's life.

POINTS TO PONDER

1. Can a professional football game be viewed as a physical "war" between two "tribes"? Can such "constructive" competition prevent or take the place of other, more deadly, "wars"? How?

2. Think of several ways physical power has been used for good purposes. Also, think of several instances where the mere threat of the use of physical power was enough to accomplish good things. Ask yourself: How have I used my physical power today?

THE BOTTOM LINE, TIP #13:

Physical power--actual or threatened--is our most basic form of power.

Power Tip #14:

ATTRACTIVENESS IS POWER

Attractive people are powerful! ("Attractiveness" here means "good-looking" physically and/or having an attractive personality. Attractiveness is more than just "skin deep.") Attractive people win much more than beauty contests; they also tend to get preferential treatment and attention.

Look at successful politicians. They usually are more attractive than opponents they have defeated in elections. That's partly why we elected them!

Studies have shown that an attractive person often is given hiring preference. Sometimes a job was offered on the spot to an attractive applicant, but not to a less attractive one with equal credentials. Likewise, a tall man is much more likely to get a job, everything else being equal.

Probably, at some level, you already know that attractive people are preferred. In fact, you probably prefer attractive people yourself. But the main question here and now is how, given your attributes, can you make yourself more attractive if you choose to do so? You can and do make that choice. You'll never be Tom Cruise, but you can be a more attractive "Joe Doakes."

A relatively new field of study called "behavioral biology" confirms all this. These researchers have shown that every society has standards of attractiveness, and that individuals meeting these standards receive preference.

Of course, standards of attractiveness vary. One society thinks fat people are attractive, and another favors thinness.

Some groups prefer thick lips; others prefer thin lips. One culture likes short hair; another likes long hair.

What, if anything, can you do about all this? Actually, a lot! You can pay attention to your physical appearance, and be sure that you are clean, becomingly clothed, and well groomed, according to the standards of the group.

Be willing to spend extra tittle and money on clothing and hair styling. You might consider employing a wardrobe consultant and having a cosmetic "make-over." When we look good, we feel better about ourselves, and about life in general. Others notice the difference; they respond positively. "Dress for Success" really works!

Of equal importance, every one of us can work on having a more attractive personality. We can learn to be more attuned to how others perceive us, and be more willing to meet their desires, if they do not conflict with our values. Generally, others like us more when we are thoughtful, interested in them, and show that we value them, even if we might disagree with them.

Chances are you already know how to make yourself more attractive. Just do it! It really will make a difference! You'll be more powerful!

POINTS TO PONDER

1. Do you think attractiveness is a fair way for you to evaluate another person? For someone else to evaluate you? Why?

2. Think of an attractive person. What about that person makes you think he or she is attractive? Why do you think those particular attributes make that person attractive? Would you be willing to give preference (such as hiring) to that person? Why?

3. Write at least three specific things you can and will do to make yourself more attractive. Include specific actions you can take to make yourself more attractive.

THE BOTTOM LINE, TIP #14:

Attractiveness is in the eye of the beholder; your success is, too!

Power Tip #15:

INFORMATION, KNOWLEDGE, AND IDEAS ARE POWER

Have you heard the terms "The Third Wave," or "The Information Age"? These terms capture much about success and power in today's advanced societies.

In the "First Wave" societies principally were based on hunting and farming. Next came the "Second Wave," sometimes called the "Industrial Revolution." Then came the "Third Wave," where the "cutting edges" of societies are based on the "Information Revolution," or the "Information Age." We now are in the "Information Age."

The implications of these changing "Ages" or technologies are profound. For example, in the "First Wave," based on hunting and farming, the dominant issue was using human physical strength (power) effectively. Generally, a person was successful or not based upon how well he or she used his or her physical strength.

In the "Second Wave," or the "Industrial Revolution," success or failure generally shifted to the "means of production," and the capital (money) to buy them. Fortunes were made from factories that largely used machines driven by energy (power) from fossil fuels. Individuals depended upon their personal trade or skill.

Now, in "The Third Wave," success or failure (our power) depends more upon how much we know and how well we manipulate data with computers. Perhaps the importance of The Third Wave is dramatized by the fact that the world's wealthiest person--Bill Gates--made his fortune by creating computer software programs with his Microsoft Corporation.

I am writing this book using a computer with a word processing program. Several years ago, when I wrote other books, I laboriously wrote them by hand. Then I hired a typist to put the material into good form. Now I have no need for a typist; I'm typing on a computer as I think. For me, the typist is obsolete. Multiply my situation by millions of similar ones, and a whole skill--typing--has been practically eliminated as a primary job description. Some former typists, of course, have "graduated" to become word processing specialists.

Somewhat surprisingly, studies of students who majored in business administration in college have shown that, after graduating and working in their career field, they thought their most valuable course in college was (Surprise!) "Report Writing"! Not really too surprising when you stop and think about it, however. What could be more important in modern business than the ability to clearly communicate in writing?

Truly, what you don't know or can't communicate can hurt you!

POINTS TO PONDER

1. How well are you prepared to succeed in "The Third Wave"? What things do you need to do to upgrade important skills?

2. Does "The Third Wave" completely eliminate physical strength and mechanization? Or do these factors continue to be present, but perhaps in some ways be overshadowed by "The Third Wave"?

3. What sort of career preparation would you suggest for your children or grandchildren. How does this differ from your own preparation?

The Bottom Line, Tip #15:
Catch "The Third Wave," while you can.

Power Tip #16:

YOUR "TRIBES" ARE POWER

Why do you...	It's because you, in large measure, have adopted the standards of...
Dress like you do?	one of your tribes.
Eat like you do?	one of your tribes.
Worship like you do?	one of your tribes.
Talk like you do?	one of your tribes.
Work like you do?	one of your tribes.
Think like you do?	one of your tribes.
Spend money like you do?	one of your tribes.
Love like you do?	one of your tribes.
Do many, many other things the way you do?	one of your tribes.

The history of humans largely is written in terms of the physical territories over which "human tribes" physically fought. Tribal wars were (and are!) major factors in almost everyone's life.

Two tribes fight over the hunting rights between two rivers. A crusade is launched hundreds of years ago to conquer infidels, who had conquered other "tribes," who had conquered still other "tribes." Today, a missile attack is launched in response to military action by another "tribe."

"Tribes?", you ask. Didn't modern life do away with tribes? No, it didn't; our modern tribes are just dressed in new uniforms. When you insist on wearing a certain brand of shoes approved by your peer group, that's "tribal" behavior. "Cool" used to refer only to temperature. Now "cool" also means correct or approved behavior. Who made this change? A "tribe" did.

Your tribes give you an identity and a sense of belonging. Your tribes prescribe your values, tastes, and behaviors. Your tribes tell you what is right and what is wrong. Your tribes tell you when you succeed and when you fail. Your religions, laws, ordinances, rules, and regulations are set by your tribes. Truly, your tribes are your extended family.

We wear the uniforms of our tribes, whether it's a certain brand of sneakers, a sports team uniform, or a high-fashion gown. In Siena, Italy, there is a horse race each year sponsored by the ancient tribes of the city. Beginning immediately after a race, the whole year is spent preparing for the next race. On the day of the race, every citizen wears or displays the ancient uniforms and colors of his or her tribe.

Perhaps more than you have realized it, you are a product of your tribes. And your behavior is in large measure determined by your tribes. To be well-thought-of by your peers probably is one of your most powerful motivators.

We all are familiar with "peer pressure," and most--perhaps, all of us have had serious conflicts about it. If your school friends smoked cigarettes (or "pot") did you feel pressure to go along with them and also smoke?

One marriage partner grew up in the "country club" set. But she married a "ski-bum." For a while the marriage prospered, but then the inevitable conflicts emerged. Which was more important, going skiing or going to the country club?

Is one ethnic group or race better than others? Is God more on the side of one race than another? Is my football team better than yours?

Of course, in modern, complex life you probably are a member of many tribes that often prescribe conflicting behaviors for you. Attempting to resolve such conflicts might make your problems and their solutions more complicated than if you had been a member of an early human tribe. For millions of years hunter-gatherer tribes of about 50 to 100 members made up the human organization- -that is, the tribe. Even then, things changed, but at a much slower rate than now.

We might like to think that we've "progressed" beyond our tribes. But have we? In many important respects, "no." Our tribes still have profound influences on us. Our tribes give us our values, our identity, our goals, and our behaviors.

POINTS TO PONDER

1. Think of at least six "tribes" of which you are a member. Are many of your conflicts due to conflicting standards prescribed for you by your tribes?

2. How much of your, my, and the world's problems are due to "tribal" behavior? What can you do to help?

3. Have you ever been "thrown out" of any of your

tribes? Why? How did you resolve the conflicts involved?
Have you ever quit any of your tribes? Were there painful
consequences?

4. In the United States we are having a vigorous debate
about "family values." Political, moral, ethical, and
religious values are involved. Each is promoted by its
tribe. Where do you stand on these issues? How do your
tribes influence you on these matters?

5. Try to imagine what your life would be like without
tribes. Would it be better or worse? Why? Would your
life have any meaning at all without your tribes? How can
you be an individual and at the same time belong to your
tribes? Is this difficult? Why?

The Bottom Line, Tip #16:

Choose your tribes carefully; they largely will run your life.

Power Tip #17:

ORGANIZATIONS ARE POWER

Most human power is in organizations.

You create--in a sense out of "thin air"--an organization, "willing" it into existence by "thinking it up" and defining it. You create "some-thing"--your organization--out of "no-thing."

Next, you provide a vision for your organization. Your vision includes how others can help you achieve your and their objectives through your organization.

For example, Methvid Moore got out of bed one morning and announced to Susan, his wife, that he is forming MidCentral Airlines. MidCentral never existed before Methvid thought of it that morning. Perhaps he dreamed it. Whatever.

Every organization is formed similarly. It starts as a private thought of one person. Then it is shared with someone else. Then another step is taken. For example, Methvid goes to his bank and opens a checking account for MidCentral. Eventually, MidCentral might become the world's largest airline. (Delta Airlines grew from a crop-duster in Monroe, Louisiana.)

After defining MidCentral, Methvid gives it a vision. Without a vision an organization perishes--just like a person. Its vision is its objectives. He sets the overall vision, and he communicates it to all members.

Everyone needs to share the grand, overall vision. In addition, everyone must have a personal vision that contributes to the overall vision.

Methvid helps every member define her objectives--her vision for herself and for her part of the organization. When MidCentral becomes large, he would not personally do all of the details with every person. His managers at all levels would do this for the parts of the organization and for the members for which they are accountable.

Thinking about the "vision" and the "objectives" of an organization might sound mysterious. It's not. It's something that all good managers do. They imagine what they want their organization to be or to do.

Methvid greatly multiplied his personal power by creating and managing MidCentral, if it is successful. Would you like to multiply your power? You can, with a successful organization.

POINTS TO PONDER

1. Does any organization exist other than to accomplish objectives? Why?

2. Mahatma Ghandi, the revolutionary leader and founder of modern India, is reported to have seen a crowd rushing past his window. He is reported to have said to one of his assistants, "Go find out where they are going, for I am their leader." What does this incident tell you about how Ghandi saw the role of his people in setting his nation's and his own objectives? How is modern market research similar to this incident? Can an organization continue to exist without the support of its members--at least of its members who have significant power? Have you ever been a member of an organization that did not enjoy the support of everyone! Does it still exist?

3. What happens in an organization if it is merely assumed that everyone will automatically work to accomplish the organization's objectives? Is the role of management merely to observe passively how the organization and members perform? Why?

4. Have you ever created an organization? Have you

ever reorganized an organization? If so, how did the organization's objectives affect your work and other actions?

The Bottom Line, Tip #17:

You can multiply your personal power with organizations.

Power Tip #18:

MANAGING FOR OBJECTIVES IS POWER

You manage for objectives when you *create, define, and communicate* your organization and its objectives in terms members can understand and accept.

In Tip #17 we saw that Methvid Moore created MidCentral Airlines to accomplish some objectives. The place of "objectives" is central in forming an organization. In addition, objectives are of supreme importance in every step the organization takes, or doesn't take.

Objectives are the bases for effectively managing organizations. In fact, we can think of effective managing as "Managing for Objectives." When you stop and think about it, nothing else makes sense. Yet, losing sight of the organization's and members' objectives occurs very frequently. That is, managers often fail to "Manage for Objectives." Waste and inefficiencies result.

Methvid Moore, the founder and Chief Executive Officer (CEO) of MidCentral Airlines set, "Be the Leading Airline in the World," as MidCentral's overall objective.

The CEO's and other managers' next task is to "divide" that overall objective. This is done by breaking down and translating the overall objective into operational objectives for every component and member of your organization. The leader at every level defines and communicates objectives that will contribute to the next higher, and ultimately, the overall objective.

So, ok, you're not and probably never will be your company's CEO. What does all of this have to do with you? Everything.

You can use "Managing for Objectives" as the basis for your managing, just like Methvid did. After all, you and your workers might work for MidCentral for objectives, just like Methvid does. Only the "levels" of objectives are different. Integrating personal and organizational objectives still are of supreme importance to Methvid, you, your workers, and every other member of MidCentral.

Suppose you are Director of Sales for MidCentral's Pacific Region. Your Region's expected contribution to the overall company is to sell at least $30,000,000 during the next quarter. In addition, your sales objectives go up in each succeeding quarter.

MidCentral is an "enlightened" organization. That is, it

"Manages for Objectives." So, you fully participate with your supervisor, your subordinates, and other affected members in setting your $30,000,000 objective.

Through a similar participative process you and they set the objectives for each of your workers. For example, Jake, one of your Account Representatives, and you agree that he has an objective of $4,000,000 as his part of your Region's $30,000,000 objective.

POINTS TO PONDER

1. How well does your work organization manage for objectives? Is it clear how the various parts contribute toward the overall objectives of the organization?

2. In your work organization, is it clear how your individual work objectives contribute to the larger organization? How do you know whether or not you have done a good job? How can this process be improved?

3. My favorite quotation, by Peter Drucker, is: "The ultimate futility is to do with great efficiency that which should not be done at all." How is this statement related to "Managing for Objectives"? Does this statement say anything to you about your personal or work activities?

4. Paragon Mills has several medium-sized steel mills in the United States. Each week Paragon pays out bonuses of about 35 to 45 percent to every member of the organization. How well do you think Paragon managers and employees communicate with each other about their on-going visions or objectives for Paragon? (The answer is, of course: very, very well.) Who's the most important person in Paragon's success? Answer: Everyone, but of course, the top manager got it all started, and he keeps it going. How does your organization compare to Paragon? Would you work harder or more effectively for an extra 35 to 45 percent pay?

The Bottom Line, Tip #18:

"Managing for Objectives" just works better!

Power Tip #19:

CREATING IS POWER

Can you create creativity? You bet! You can make both yourself and your organization more creative. It's mainly a question of attitude--*your* attitude.

Have you ever thought that, to a large extent, you create your future--the "future you" and the future of your organization? You do! Other forces--over which you have limited or no control--also influence your future.

Yet, every decision you make and every action you take changes your future! Kind of a scary thought, isn't it? But, if you stop and think about it, you'll see that it's true. When you grasp that idea you can take increased responsibility for the rest of your life. Then, *you empower yourself!*

We saw earlier that Methvid Moore created MidCentral Airlines by "dreaming it up." He thought about it; he created it; he "willed" MidCentral into existence. Without Methvid, MidCentral would have continued to be--literally--nothing.

We often think that some people are creative (like Methvid) and that others are not creative. That's wrong!

Researchers have shown that *everyone is creative.* True, some people are more creative than others. But everyone can be creative, and each person's amount of being creative depends upon how you treat them, and how they treat themselves.

If they think your workers are creative and you encourage them to be creative, *they will he creative.* I guarantee it! At the same time you satisfy your own need to be creative.

I remember when I was a student in an accounting course. We were dealing with the depreciation of physical assets for a company. The instructor said, "All physical assets are on an inevitable march to the junk heap." Kind of a brutal thought, but it's true.

It's also true that almost everything your organization does is "on an inevitable march to the junk heap." That is, every thing or service your organization does will become obsolete. At least, the way it's presently done will he consigned to the junk heap.

What's the solution to such a bleak future! It's *being creative*. For long-term survival and prosperity creativity isn't optional; it's absolutely required.

When you are creative and you encourage your workers to be creative, you give yourself and your organization a new future. Add a good dose of discipline and hard work, and you might have an open road to unlimited future success.

POINTS TO PONDER

1.   To what extent does your work organization encourage and reward you for being creative? How much do you encourage and reward your workers' efforts at being creative?

2. Think of a time you, or someone else, had a brilliant idea that was accomplished. How did you and they feel about this success?

3. What are three ways you and your workers could be more creative. What hurdles will you and they have to overcome?

4.   Assume you have just learned that your major product has become obsolete. A competitor has just

patented a far superior new, replacement product. You have called a meeting of all your workers to deal with this issue. What will you do at the meeting? How will you use your workers' knowledge, experience, and creativity?

The Bottom Line, Tip #19:

Dream your dreams; that's the first step to achieving them!

Power Tip #20:

LEADING IS POWER

What or who gives life to an organization? The leader! He creates it, defines it, selects its members, and sets its overall objectives. He multiplies his and other members' power when the organization is successful.

With good leadership an organization will prosper. Without good leadership, it surely will fail. Leaders have the dominant voice in creating the organization, deciding its objectives, selecting its members, and determining how it will accomplish those objectives.

Leaders lead! They get "out in front," kind of like in the war movies. They "see" the overall picture, and they inspire others to follow. Then together they and their co-members accomplish their organizational and personal objectives.

The environment within which an organization lives is constantly changing. So the organization and its objectives must be redefined for it to continue to exist and prosper. At every step in an organization's life somebody (or somebodies) needs to redefine it, its parts, and the objectives of the whole and of every part.

Here are some of the things a leader does. He or she:

1. *Creates* the organization.

2. *Defines* the overall objectives of the organization.

3. *Plans* how the objectives will be accomplished.

4. *Selects* members.

5. *Shows* members how they can accomplish their objectives by working toward the organization's objectives.

6. *Motivates* members by sharing with them the "wealth" created by the organization. The leader supports, encourages, and inspires members.

7. *Evaluates* and *controls* the organization. How well did the organization accomplish its objectives. What changes need to be made?

An effective leader makes an organization into an integrated well-functioning whole.

Without effective leadership, an organization "goes back" to from whence it came--nothing. With effective leadership an organization can live forever (at least, a long, long, time!).

POINTS TO PONDER

1. Think of an effective, inspirational leader in your life. What attracted you to him and his organization?

2. How well is your work organization led? Are you inspired to work toward the organization's goals? Does your leader show you how you can accomplish the organization's objectives while working toward your individual, personal objectives?

3. Huey Long, once a U.S. Senator and a Governor of Louisiana, is said to have written this note to himself in the margin of one of his speeches: "Argument weak; holler like hell!" What does this tell you about leaders and their followers? Is it a human weakness that we sometimes let ourselves be led in wrong directions? Was Hitler (the leader of Nazi Germany) a good leader? Can a leader be effective without appealing to your emotions? How and why?

4. What can you do to be a more effective leader in your work organization? Do you want and are you willing to do these things?

The Bottom Line, Tip #20:

A leader converts his, your, and my objectives into our objective. Lead, follow, or get out!

Power Tip #21:

BE POWERFUL; CREATE YOUR FUTURE

A funny thing happened on the way to your future. *You created it*! *Who* created it? *You* did! Yes, that's right, *you* did! Your future will be what it becomes partly--perhaps largely--because of what you did or didn't do between now and then.

What's at stake here? Simply, the remainder your life. That's big! You have the power to choose and create your future, at least to a large extent. When you make successful choices, you become more powerful.

Sometimes you will fail. But if you pick yourself up, dust yourself off, and climb back onto the challenge of being responsible for your life, you will, I think, be much more successful and satisfied with yourself and your life, than if you just passively "go along."

We hear a lot about taking personal responsibility for our actions or inactions. And, often it seems easier to just "go with the flow." That's fine if "the flow" takes you where you want to go. But, chances are it often won't.

You can and do change your future. If you don't like the way your future looks, change it! (At the minimum, you certainly at least can change your attitude!) In fact you're the only person who, for sure, *can* change your future. Others will affect your future, but only if you choose to let them or place yourself in a position where they can affect you. (I've affected your present and future because you're reading my book! And, of course, there are situations and forces over which none of us has any control.)

You affect your organizations by the decisions you make. The visions you have for yourself and your organizations are extremely important. Your life, the lives of others, and the lives of your organizations are at stake.

Take personal responsibility for the rest of your life! You can do that; nobody else or no other organization can do that as well as you can.

Create, define, inspire, light fires to, and empower yourself and others. Hundreds of people might be needed to push "the boulder up the mountain and keep it there," with more strength than they ever used or thought they had. Maybe, for you, "pushing the boulder up the mountain" means increasing your organization's sales to $12,000,000 per year. What is your challenge?

Your future will be, in part, what you created. Imagine where you want yourself and your organizations to go. Then go there.

POINTS TO PONDER

1. Identify a problem or issue in your personal life or in one of your organizations. Are you willing to be personally responsible for making the decisions and taking the consequences of your decisions to resolve this matter? What resistances or fears do you have about dealing with this issue? What can you do about them?

2. Are you more active or more passive when you have tough problems to solve? What part of you, if any, would you like to change about this?

3. Think of a decision you made that clearly "created your future." How do you feel about this decision and its consequences? Are you willing to do more of this sort of thing? Why?

The Bottom Line, Tip #21:

You can't choose whether you will change your future, only how!